Women
of
Prayer

Women
of
Prayer

An anthology of everyday prayers
from women around the world

COMPILED BY DOROTHY STEWART

Loyola Press

Chicago

Loyola Press

3441 North Ashland Avenue
Chicago, Illinois 60657

First North American edition: 1999

Interior design by Amy Evans McClure
Art by Meltem Aktas

Library of Congress Cataloging-in-Publication Data
Women of prayer : an anthology of everyday prayers from women
    around the world / compiled by Dorothy Stewart. — 1st ed.

     p.   cm.
   Includes index.
   ISBN 0-8294-1280-8
   1. Prayers. 2. Women—Prayer-books and devotions—English.
I. Stewart, Dorothy M.
BV283.W6W65 1999
242'.643—dc21   98-28274
                                               CIP

Printed in the United States of America
99 00 01 02 03 / 10 9 8 7 6 5 4 3 2 1

To my family and friends:
almost without exception
women of prayer

Contents

Forgive me   28

PART TWO: *Everyday Lives*

Our lives in God's hand

The day ahead

For families, friends, and neighbors 115

When life is hard 124

Help us to help others 134

PART THREE: *The Wider World*

For creation

A Word from the Compiler

Women have always been great pray-ers. Though few published anthologies include many prayers by women, women have been quietly writing their prayers all along. My problem has not been finding prayers by women, but rather making the final choice from the unimaginable riches I discovered.

Many of the prayers in this collection are contemporary, written by women alive now. A smaller number are from women of past ages. Some prayers are one-liners, and others are longer and more reflective. Some were written for public occasions and some for private use.

Part One, "Women and God," lays the groundwork—women's relationship with God. These are prayers of trust and hope, forgiveness and devotion; the prayers that underpin faith and life.

Part Two, "Everyday Lives," samples the enormous range of experiences and concerns in our daily lives. Here are prayers about work and friends, our families and ourselves, our sorrows and our joys. These prayers show that we can take *any* situation to God, no matter how terrible or trivial, because God cares about *all* areas of life.

Part Three, "The Wider World," includes an international selection of prayers drawn largely from the annual Women's World Day of Prayer services. These prayers express our concerns for peace and justice and for an end to oppression, pollution, and exploitation. As we pray them, we recognize our responsibility for our world as partners with God in creation.

I hope that there is something in this anthology for every woman. Even more, I hope that praying these prayers will deepen our relationship with God, who waits lovingly to hear from each of us.

Dorothy Stewart

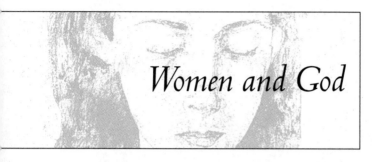

PART ONE

Women and God

These are prayers of women's personal experience of God:
  prayers of hope
      —and prayers expressing the need for hope,
  prayers of faith
      —and prayers asking for faith,
  prayers of love and trust, thanks and praise
      —and prayers expressing the fundamental step
        of wanting to pray, needing to pray, but not
        knowing how to start.

Lord, teach us to pray.

Teach me to pray

A friend who listens

O teach me to pray, Lord.
Teach me to pray.
I need someone to talk to,
A friend Who will listen,
I need hope,
Refreshment.
What were those words I used to know?
"You will find a solace there."
Can He mean me, O praise Him!
But what can I say?
O teach me to pray, Lord.
Teach me to pray.

Jean Bryan

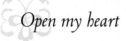

Open my heart

Dear Lord, I open my heart to your coming. Come close to me, Lord, and let me yield my whole being to you. Teach me to know myself and to fill my empty being with the radiant life of your love, that I may become a fountain of blessing to quench my own thirsts and to offer love to meet the thirsts of my companions on this journey to you.

Susan Coupland

God of the open spaces

Lord of the field,
Lord of the wind,
Christ Jesus, Intercessor,
teach us to pray.

Amy Carmichael (1868–1951)

Still my heart

Settle my silly heart, good Lord.
Hold me still in your motherly embrace,
enfolded by your wings of peace and love,
and total acceptance. Soothe me,
love me into peace,
like a weaned child snuggled
in trust on her mother's lap.
So hold me, Lord,
and let us enjoy this time together.
Speak to my heart if you will,
but most of all be present to me,
and me to you.

Dorothy Stewart

Loving like a mother, trusting like a child

Mother me, my Father,
That I may step unbowed
From safe within your haven
To face a hostile crowd.

Mother me, my Father,
And help to ease the pain
Of taunts and tears and teasing
And make me love again.

Mother me, my Father,
With hands so deeply scarred,
That I may touch some other
Whose suffering is hard.

Mother me, my Father,
That all my life be styled
On loving like a mother
And trusting like a child.

Helena McKinnon

Embrace this soul of mine

Ah, dear love of God, always embrace this soul of mine,
For it pains me above all things
When I am separated from you.
Ah, love, do not allow me to grow cool
For all my works are dead
When I can feel you no longer.

Saint Mechtild of Magdeburg (ca. 1207–ca. 1292)

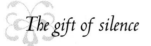 *The gift of silence*

We are so busy, Lord, we do not listen.
The world is so noisy, Lord, we do not hear.
We do not hear what your Spirit is saying to each one of us.
We have been afraid of silence.
Lord, teach us to use your gift of silence.
Teach us, Lord.

Women of New Zealand

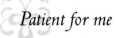

Patient for me

Angle my life, O fisher-God,
And bait my mind,
For I had struggled to evade your rod
And sought to find
A peace outside the rulings of your sea,
Outside your claim. . . .
But you were patient and would wait for me
Until I came.

Kate Compston

An open invitation

Lord, you invite us—
not some of us,
all of us:
not the good and righteous,
all of us—
unconditionally.

Lord, we come—
meeting you,
meeting each other,
accepting each other,
unconditionally.

Lord, we go—
constant in prayer, and prayerful action,
expressing your continuous invitation—
loving, sharing,
seeking, bringing,
serving the world you love.

> *Women's World Day of Prayer*
> *International Executive Committee*

Like the trees of the forest

Great and Merciful God,

As the trees of the forest grow straight and tall reaching up their branches towards the heavens drinking in your gifts of sunshine and rain, help us to reach out towards you, to accept your gifts of love and mercy, to grow in grace and to live and die in your love.

Alison O'Grady

Speechless in prayer

O Lord, my heart is all a prayer,
But it is silent unto Thee;
I am too tired to look for words,
I rest upon Thy sympathy
To understand when I am dumb,
And well I know Thou hearest me.

Amy Carmichael (1868–1951)

The quiet hills of prayer

Father, forgive us that we are often too busy or too lazy
to go up into the hills of prayer—
to high ground where we might meet you.

Forgive us that when we do carve out a space for prayer
we become easily distracted or drowsy
and are unaware of your nearness.

Thank you, then, especially thank you
that your grace so often waits on our slowness.

Kate Compston

Behind closed doors

Lord, give me the joy of private praying. Keep me faithful to shut the door every day and spend time with You and Your Word in secret. Teach me to draw apart alone with You, no matter where I am or with whom.

Evelyn Christenson

The peace of God

Jesus, Lord, you come to us
not as we come to you—
with excuses, bluster, bewilderment,
and a million petitions.
You come to us in peace.
You come to us with peace.
Lord, let your peace
be alive in my life, today.

Dorothy Stewart

Influence my thoughts

Think through me, thoughts of God;
My Father, quiet me,
Till in Thy holy presence, hushed,
I think Thy thoughts with Thee.

Think through me, thoughts of God,
That always, everywhere,
The stream that through my being flows
May homeward pass in prayer.

Think through me, thoughts of God,
And let my own thoughts be
Lost like the sand pools on the shore
Of the eternal sea.

Amy Carmichael (1868–1951)

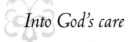# Into God's care

Lord God, I bring to you:
- —My sins for your forgiveness.
- —My hopes, my aims, my ambitions for your blessings.
- —My temptations for your strength.
- —My words and duties and responsibilities for your help.
- —My family, friends and all loved ones for your care and protection.
- —My sickness for your healing.

Women of Kenya

Strengthen us

Spirit of purity and grace,
our weakness pitying see;
O make our hearts thy dwelling place,
and worthier of thee.

Harriet Auber (1773–1862)

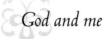

God and me

You are God.
You are here.
Your Spirit is with me.
Thank you, God.

Dorothy Stewart

The shores of my life

Come beachcomber spirit
search the shores
    of my life;
bring to remembrance
love's presence.

Sister Gillian Mary

Every hour of every day

I need Thee every hour, most gracious Lord;
No tender voice like Thine can peace afford.

I need Thee every hour, stay Thou near by;
Temptations lose their power when Thou art nigh.

I need Thee every hour, in joy or pain;
Come quickly and abide, or life is vain.

I need Thee every hour, teach me Thy will,
And Thy rich promises in me fulfill.

I need Thee every hour, most Holy One;
O make me Thine indeed, Thou blessed Son.

Annie Sherwood Hawks (1835–1918)

Just as I am

Just as I am, without one plea
but that thy blood was shed for me,
and that thou bidst me come to thee,
O Lamb of God, I come.

Just as I am, though tossed about
with many a conflict, many a doubt,
fightings and fears within, without,
O Lamb of God, I come.

Just as I am, thou wilt receive,
wilt welcome, pardon, cleanse, relieve,
because thy promise I believe,
O Lamb of God, I come.

Charlotte Elliott (1789–1871)

A love to meet all needs

O Savior, I have naught to plead
In earth beneath or heaven above,
But just my own exceeding need,
And Thy exceeding love.

Jane Crewdson (1809–1863)

Searching

Here I am, O Lord, in search of myself,
    that I may find life's meaning and purpose
    for me in my age and circumstance.
Lord, show me myself.

Here I am, O Lord, in search of my neighbors
    through their needs, frustrations and hopes.
Lord, show me my neighbors.

Here I am, O Lord, in search of You
    as I search for myself and my neighbors.
Lord, show me Yourself.

Women of Jamaica

A light in the darkness

Holy Spirit,
mighty wind of God,
inhabit our darkness
brood over our abyss
and speak to our chaos;
that we may breathe with your life
and share your creation
in the power of Jesus Christ.
Amen.

Janet Morley

In you is all

God, of your goodness, give me yourself;
   for you are enough for me.
I cannot properly ask anything less, to be worthy of you.
If I were to ask less, I should always be in want.
In you alone do I have all.

Julian of Norwich (1342–ca. 1416)

Forgive me

No limits

Lord, I know there are no limits to your love
   or to the invitation to share its power—but I create limits.
I want to love and serve other people in your name,
   but then—I am too timid, too uncertain, too proud.
I am unwilling to take risks, to venture into unfamiliar
      situations
   because I cannot see you there.
I judge others as I see them, by my standards and not yours,
   forgetting that I could never be worthy
   of your amazing love for me.
Lord, have mercy upon me and forgive my sin.

Women's World Day of Prayer
International Executive Committee

Unconditional love

Thank you, Lord,
for loving me when I am my most unlovable.
Give me love enough to love others as you love me.

Kathy Keay

Forgive our selfishness

Lord, we're sorry that we sometimes love you selfishly. We look to your words and actions to confirm our own opinions and we follow you for what we can get from you. Please help us to follow the *real* you and not the God of our fears and fantasies.

Alison White

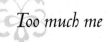

Too much me

Lord God,
there is so much me in me.
Let there be less me in me,
and more you.

Dorothy Stewart

Looking to the light

Crazy, really—to prefer darkness to light,
    the cold to the warmth.
Yet so often that's what we choose,
    what I choose.
And suffer the regrets
    afterwards.
Help me choose light, Lord Jesus.
Strengthen me to choose *You*.

Dorothy Stewart

A plea

Show me what's wrong with my life! I can't get through to You!

Evelyn Christenson

Forgive our failure

We fail You when we should hope, but are discouraged;
When we should trust, but are distrustful;
When we should act, but are hesitant;
When we should be eager, but are complacent;
When we should rejoice, but are sad.

Lord, Whose mercy never fails,
    We thank You for everything we have received:
bread and life, work and health, hope and achievement,
    and for the miracle of human love.
Lord, Whose mercy never fails,
    We take refuge in You and Your faithfulness.

Women of East Germany

Break us, remake us

O Wind of God, come, bend us, break us,
till humbly we confess our need;
then in your tenderness remake us,
revive, restore; for this we plead.

Bessie Porter Head (1850–1936)

A spirit of power and love

Heavenly Father, we thank you that you have given us a spirit of power and love, yet we confess that we are often filled with a spirit of fear, and instead of having your peace within us there is anxiety and turmoil. Forgive us for our lack of trust, and help us to be more aware of your presence with us.

Women's World Day of Prayer
International Executive Committee

Strength to live the words we say

"Forgive our sins as we forgive,"
   you taught us, Lord, to pray,
but you alone can grant us grace
   to live the words we say.

How can your pardon reach and bless
   the unforgiving heart
that broods on wrongs and will not let
   old bitterness depart?

In blazing light your Cross reveals
   the truth we dimly knew:
what trivial debts are owed to us,
   how great our debt to you!

Lord, cleanse the depths within our souls
   and bid resentment cease.
Then, bound to all in bonds of love,
   our lives will spread your peace.

Rosamond E. Herklots (1905–1987)

Cleanse me, heal me

Lord,
you know the searchings of my heart.
You listen with love and concern to my cares.
Hear my heart's sorrows, and heal, O Lord.
Cleanse away all my transgressions,
heal my wounds,
and set me on my feet to serve you.

Dorothy Stewart

Forward in prayer

O lead us on—weigh not our merits,
For we have none to weigh.
But, Savior, pardon our offenses.
Lead even us today
Further in the way of prayer,
Holy Spirit, lead us there.

Amy Carmichael (1868–1951)

Open our eyes and ears

Lord, we confess that we have failed often. In our anxiety that You should listen to us we have not listened to You.

Lord, forgive our ways.

In our concern for our own families we have shown too little care for those of others. Lest our pattern of life be upset, we have hesitated to become involved in the difficulties of others.

Lord, forgive and direct our coming days.

Through not living close enough to You we have failed to show the joy of living.

Lord, forgive, so may we give You praise.

Keep us, Lord, from the jealousy which wounds others,
the self-will which causes hurt to others,
the self-pity which blinds us to the needs of others.

Women of New Zealand

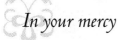
In your mercy

Lord, hear; Lord, forgive; Lord, do.
Hear what I speak not,
forgive what I speak amiss,
do what I leave undone;
that, not according to my word or my deed,
but according to Thy mercy and truth,
all may issue to Thy glory
and the good of Thy Kingdom. Amen.

Maria Hlare (nineteenth century)

Freed from the burden of care

God strengthen me to bear myself;
That heaviest weight of all to bear,
Inalienable weight of care.

If I could once lay down myself,
And start self-purged upon the race
That all must run! Death runs apace.

If I could set aside myself,
And start with lightened heart upon
The road by all men overgone!

God harden me against myself,
This coward with pathetic voice
Who craves for ease, and rest and joys;

Myself, archtraitor to myself,
My hollowest friend, my deadliest foe,
My clog whatever road I go.

Yet One there is can curb myself,
Can roll the strangling load from me,
Break off the yoke and set me free.

Christina Rossetti (1830–1894)

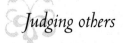
Judging others

Lord Jesus, help us to see our own faults
more clearly than the faults of others.

Beryl Bye

Strength within

I feel that I am weak,
And prone to every sin;
But Thou who gives to those who seek,
Wilt give me strength within.

I need not fear my foes,
I need not yield to care,
I need not sink beneath my woes,
For Thou wilt answer prayer.

In my Redeemer's Name
I give myself to Thee;
And, all unworthy as I am,
My God will cherish me.

Anne Brontë (1820–1849)

Just one request . . .

O God we ask one favor,
that we may be forgiven.

Emily Dickinson (1830–1886)

Thanks and praise

The power and the glory

Eternal God,
>you are the power that created the universe,
>the energy that fires everything,
>the strength that sustains our world.

Eternal Father,
>you are the love that encircles us,
>the grace that enables us,
>the truth that enlightens us.

Eternal Savior,
>you are the glory of the cross of Christ,
>the hope of the resurrection,
>the life of the Holy Spirit.

God of love, power and might.

Anne Knighton

More than we can dream of

We thank you, God
   because you give us
   more than we would ever dream of asking:
   daily bread and shared meals that become feasts,
   the breath of life and voices to celebrate,
   the understanding of our history
   and the hope of our future.
   Work we can do, and time to be recreated,
   people to love and trust,
   people who love and trust us,
   gifts and responsibilities.
We thank you, God
   because you ask of us
   more than we dream of giving:
   skills we have never developed,
   care for a world whose problems we cannot solve,
   listening which hurts us,
   giving which leaves us empty-handed,
   love which makes us vulnerable,
   faith which seems impossible.

But you do not ask us to be supermen and women.
    You challenge us to be human.
Give us the courage to be human
    because you yourself became human
    and lived our lives,
    knowing our imperfections,
    sharing our joy and pain,
    making us your people
    so that we can say together,
"Our Father . . ."

Jan S. Pickard

The source of all love

Lord, you are my lover,
My longing,
My flowing stream,
My sun,
And I am your reflection.

Saint Mechtild of Magdeburg (ca. 1207–ca. 1292)

Master of my life

Lord and Master of my life,
Owner of my every minute,
I thank Thee.

Amy Carmichael (1868–1951)

Lord of heaven and earth

You are the King of Glory,
you are the Prince of Peace,
you are the Lord of heaven and earth,
you're the Sun of Righteousness.
Angels bow down before you,
worship and adore;
for you have the words of eternal life,
you are Jesus Christ the Lord.
Hosanna to the Son of David!
Hosanna to the King of kings!
Glory in the highest heaven,
for Jesus the Messiah reigns!

Mavis Ford
© *Springtime/Word Music (UK)/CopyCare Ltd. 1978*

A psalm of thanks

We thank you, God!
We want to tell the world
what you have done:
your wonderful works.
We praise you, God!
We remember our beginnings
and celebrate belonging
together in your world.
We trust you, God!
You are still our help.
We go forward in faith
remembering all you have done.

Jan S. Pickard
a paraphrase of Psalm 105:1–5

Trusting God

Help us to trust

Thank you, Lord, that beneath the surface of human power,
   chaos and uncontrollable events,
you can be found,
   quietly working out your deep and far-reaching plans.
Help us to trust you more.

   Angela Reith

God in charge

Lord, guide.
I know you're in charge.
And I thank you for your love and care for us,
and for the love of your people.

Dorothy Stewart

 *Abide in peace*

Be Thou my understanding: thus shall I know that which it may please Thee that I should know. Nor will I henceforth weary myself with seeking: but I will abide in peace with Thine understanding which shall wholly occupy my mind. I will not turn my eyes except towards Love. There will I stay and not move. I see all good to be in Thee. My spirit can find no place but Thee for its repose. . . . O God! I do not wish to follow Thee for Thy gifts! I want Thyself alone! I want nothing but Thee alone!

Saint Catherine of Genoa (1447–1510)

This endless list

This endless list;
Energy spent worrying over things best left in your care.
Lord, teach me to leave them there.

Rosemary Atkins

# A childlike trust

Help me let go of trying—
help me be Your child.

Dorothy Stewart

Praying in faith

O God our Father,
may we have the faith to expect answers to our prayers.

Beryl Bye

Beyond ourselves

Lord of the unexpected moment,
Christ the surprising,
　　why do we always
　　try to own you,
　　mistake reality for dream,
　　shut the door on the impossible?

Calm our fears,
shatter the walls we build
　　to keep you out.
Confront our hypocrisy.
Catch us when we fail.
Son of God,
Save us from ourselves.

　　Kate McIlhagga

Eternal designs

I do not know, O God, what may happen to me today. I only
know that nothing will happen to me but what has been fore-
seen by you from all eternity, and that is sufficient, O my God,
to keep me in peace. I adore your eternal designs. I submit to
them with all my heart. I desire them all and accept them all.
I make a sacrifice of everything. I unite this sacrifice to that of
your dear Son, my Savior, begging you by his infinite merits, for
the patience in troubles, and the perfect submission which is
due to you in all that you will and design for me.

Madame Elizabeth of France (1764–1794)
written while in prison awaiting the guillotine

Thou art life

Lord, Thou art life, though I be dead:
Love's fire Thou art, however cold I be:
Nor heaven have I, nor place to lay my head,
Nor home, but Thee.

Christina Rossetti (1830–1894)

Trusting in God's love

I love you, God, I trust you, I believe in you, I need you now.

Mother Teresa of Calcutta (1910–1997)

A strong tower

Merciful God, be Thou now unto us a strong tower of defense.
Give us grace to await Thy leisure, and patiently to bear what
Thou doest unto us, nothing doubting Thy goodness towards
us. Therefore do with us all things as thou wilt: Only arm us,
we beseech Thee, with Thy armor, that we may stand fast; above
all things taking to us the shield of faith, praying always that we
may refer ourselves wholly to Thy will, being assuredly persuaded
that all Thou doest cannot but be well. And unto Thee be all
honor and glory.

Lady Jane Grey (1537–1554)
written while in prison

Strength of my heart

Strength of my heart, I need not fail,
Not mine to fear but to obey.
With such a Leader who could quail?
Thou art as Thou wert yesterday.
Strength of my heart, I rest in Thee,
Fulfill Thy Purposes through me.

Amy Carmichael (1868–1951)

The way of God

Lord, it seems that what I had is gone.
But you remain—my King and Shepherd.
I will make a new way for you;
I will find my way in you.
But I am tired and powerless:
   come to me in your power and carry me
   close to your heart.

Jenny Petersen

Seeing things God's way

Father . . .

    keep us so close to Your heart
    that even our dreams are peaceful,
    and that we may see things . . .
    more and more from Your point of view.

Corrie ten Boom (1892–1983)

What should I do?

Lead us

Fire of the Spirit—
    moving and loving—
warm us and lead us,
    encourage and change us.

Fire of the Spirit—
    give light to our chaos,
drive out our confusions
    and heal our hurt world.

Fire of the Spirit—
    join us together,
dance in our churches,
    transform our lives.

Jan S. Pickard

A question . . .

Here I am, Lord—inquiring of you.
Please, is there an answer?

Dorothy Stewart

Doing God's will

Dear Father God, I believe that I am where I am because You
have put me here. Help me to stay here and work for You, until
You make clear that You want me to be somewhere else.

Beryl Bye

Called by name

On Isaiah 49:16, "I have written your name on the palms of my hands."

Lord, we know our own names:
labeled, passported, well-documented:
we know who we are and where we are going.
But we are still anxious, restless,
constantly checking our labels:
do we know who we are
and where we are going?
You do not label us, but call us by name,
love us, and hold our lives in your hand:
help us to know we are loved
and to trust in you as we go.

Jan S. Pickard

Alive in the light

Don't let me go back to the dark, please, Lord!
O let me live in the light!

Arulai of Dohnavur

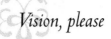

Vision, please

Lord, help me to see!

Dorothy Stewart

Transformation

Molded by God's love

Lord,
 let your love search me and know me,
 let your love shine upon me and cleanse me from sin,
 let your love heal me and transform me,
 let your love strengthen me and inspire me,
 let your love direct me in your service,
In Jesus' name. Amen.

Dorothy Stewart

Partners in transformation

O God, you claim me as your partner,
   respecting me,
   trusting me,
   tussling with me.
Support me
   as I dare to be vulnerable with you,
encourage me
   as I dare take risks with you,
so together we can transform our world. Amen.

Bridget Rees

A stumbling beginner

Lord,
I am a stumbling beginner,
    unconfident,
    unused to trusting,
    afraid to trust.
Please help me.

I'm also pigheaded—I'm stubborn and want my own way!
Please forgive me and overcome that in me.
But you know that, don't you?
And you're still prepared to take me on and work with me.

Wonderful Lord!

Dorothy Stewart

 *Shine in me*

Lord,
Let the glow of Thy great love
Through my whole being shine.

Amy Carmichael (1868–1951)

A candle in my heart

O great Chief,
light a candle within my heart
that I may see what is therein
and sweep the rubbish from your dwelling place.

An African girl

Set me free

O Lord my God, I hope in Thee;
My dear Lord Jesus, set me free;
In chains, in pains,
I long for Thee.
On bended knee
I adore Thee, implore Thee
To set me free.

Mary, Queen of Scots (1542–1587)
written while in prison

Remade through forgiveness

Almighty God,
Who knows all our dark secrets and hidden purposes,
cause the light of Your forgiving love to shine in our hearts,
so that our lives become clean and open.

Beryl Bye

Learning to grow

Lord Jesus, Rabbi, Teacher,
thank you for reminding us
that until we bring you our darkness
    we cannot know your light;
that until we become the servants of truth
    we cannot become wise leaders;
that until we are good listeners
    we cannot speak with authority;
that until we become willing, lifelong learners
    we cannot teach with insight or enthusiasm;
that until we are ready to be reborn
    we cannot truly mature.

Kate Compston

You ask too much, you give so much

O my Lord, you ask too much.
"All" is such a little word to say
but it has roots at many points
like bramble. When I think
I've dug up everything and handed it to you
I find another shoot that I've held back—
my Lord.

O my Lord, you ask too much.
Leave me just one illusion, one boast,
one single little sin that holds some warmth,
one small indulgence, one bit of flattery,
one harmless moan, one moment of my own,
one memory, one dream, one silly hope . . .
my Lord.

O my Lord, you ask too much.
To ask of Christ was one thing:
he was a part of you, and had his mind
fixed so unwaveringly on you. . . .

To ask of me is quite another,
torn as I am and hesitant—
my Lord.

O my Lord, you give so much.
If I could find the faith to offer back
all that I am to you, you'd fill
the void of my uprooted schemes,
relinquished hopes, surrendered dreams,
with more than I have asked or known . . .
my Lord.

O my Lord, you give so much.
Help me to trust you for the wealth
you're holding out to me, the light
you offer for my darkness, crown
for cross. . . . Give me the mind of Christ
that I may offer all at last—
my Lord, my God, my Life.

Kate Compston

Your will be done

The desire to follow God

I desire one thing only—the accomplishment of Thy will in me and through me. I follow and desire more and more to follow one end alone—the gaining of Thy greater glory by the realization of Thy designs for me.

Elisabeth Leseur (1866–1914)

Instruction needed!

Lord,
tell me what you want me to do,
where you want me to go,
how you want me to do it.

Evelyn Christenson

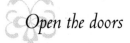 # Open the doors

O God, I want only Your will in my life. Open the doors You have for me, and give me the courage and faith to go through them.

Evelyn Christenson

Your will in my life

Let me not be wasted, Lord.
Let me grow to my full stature.
Not irritate, lacerate, dictate,
But create, be created, O Creator.

Jean Lamb

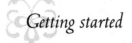

Getting started

O Lord God, give me grace this very day really and truly to begin, for what I have done till now is nothing. . . .

Mother Teresa of Calcutta (1910–1997)

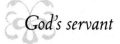 *God's servant*

Reign in my heart.
Reign in my will.
Reign in my thoughts and in my purposes.
Use me for Thine own ends of love and mercy.
Here am I; send me.

Olive Wyon

Strength to serve

I do earnestly entreat Thee, that to the very last I may never
deny Thee, or in any way have my life or conversation inconsis-
tent with my love to Thee and most earnest desire to live to Thy
glory: for I have loved Thee, O Lord, and desired to serve Thee
without reserve. Be entreated, that through Thy faithfulness,
and the power of Thy own Spirit, I may serve Thee unto the
end. Amen.

Elizabeth Fry (1780–1845)

Following the path

Lord, who forgives,
give me clear sight
and feet that walk your path
for ever.

Dorothy Stewart

No turning back

O God,
because of my free choice
and for the sake of Your love alone,
I want to remain here
and do what Your will demands of me.
No. I will not turn back.

Mother Teresa of Calcutta (1910–1997)

Take my will

And shall I pray, Oh, change Thy will, my Father,
Until it be according unto mine?
Ah no, Lord, no, that never could be, rather
I pray Thee, Blend my human will with Thine.
And work in me to will and do Thy pleasure,
Let all within me, peaceful, reconciled,
Tarry content my Well-Beloved's leisure
At last, at last, even as a wearied child.

Amy Carmichael (1868–1951)

Steer the ship of my life

Lord, I want you to steer the ship of my life.
Help me to trust your navigation,
to follow your way, not my own.

Jane Grayshon

Forgive my lack of faith

Lord, forgive me for all the times my lack of faith has burst out in exasperation, frustration, despair, anger. Help me to see where you are at work in my life. Show me *your* priorities and help me make them my priorities. Let me walk your way!

Dorothy Stewart

Renew us

O God, our very humanity makes us easy victims of our temptations. The attractive, undisciplined ways of our world weaken our resolve to choose always the "better part." Renew Your Spirit within us, we pray, so that day by day we may make the right choices.

Women of Australia

Wholehearted love

Teach me, O Lord,
to love Thee with my whole heart,
to desire nothing but Thy will,
to be content for ever in Thy Presence.

Marjorie Milne (1907–1977)

All that I need

Lord, here I am.

There is no friction between my will and Yours. Whatever You have for me, I know that You will give me enough strength, enough grace. I know You will give me all that I need, so Lord, here I am, ready to do Your will.

Evelyn Christenson

Work in us

Take our tongues and speak through them.
Take our hands and work with them.
Take our hearts and set them on fire with love for You.
In Your Name we ask it.
Amen.

Beryl Bye

PART TWO

Everyday Lives

The seasons of a woman's life bring an enormous range of experiences. Here are prayers reflecting many of these—
    the world of work outside and inside the home,
    life with family, friends, and neighbors,
    greeting new life and saying farewell,
    times of sorrow and times of rejoicing.
Women through the centuries have prayed their way through these experiences, bringing their worries and joys to God. With them, let us share our everyday lives and concerns with God in prayer.

Our lives in God's hand

At all times

O God, we pray that we may do Your will:

This year, as it stretches before us with all our hopes and fears, plans and projects. Help us to plan aright, and to accept Your guidance when it is shown to us, even if it means changing our preconceived ideas.

This month, as we seek to put into action some of these plans, that we may get our priorities right.

This week, if duties and pleasures rush at us clamoring for attention, or even if nothing happens that seems worthwhile.

This day, when the pressures of life can so often overwhelm us and make us forget where we are going.

This hour, when we have to act, and having acted cannot then undo what we have said and done.

This minute, as we come before You and pray to You.

May we do Your will, now and always, O Lord our God.

Women of New Zealand

Take my life

Take my life, and let it be
 consecrated, Lord, to thee;
take my moments and my days,
 let them flow in ceaseless praise.

Take my hands, and let them move
 at the impulse of thy love;
take my feet, and let them be
 swift and beautiful for thee.

Take my silver and my gold,
 not a mite would I withhold;
take my intellect, and use
 every power as thou shalt choose.

Take my will, and make it thine;
   it shall be no longer mine;
take my heart, it is thine own;
   it shall be thy royal throne.

Take my love, my Lord, I pour
   at thy feet its treasure-store;
take myself, and I will be
   ever, only, all for thee.

   Frances Ridley Havergal (1836–1879)

The day ahead

At morning light

Lord Jesus,
thank you for being this world's light.
Keep me walking in the light with you today.

Patsy Kettle

Prayer while dressing

Bless to me, O God,
    My soul and my body;
Bless to me, O God,
    My belief and my condition.

Bless to me, O God,
    My heart and my speech;
And bless to me, O God,
    The handling of my hand;

Strength and busyness of morning,
Habit and temper of modesty,
Force and wisdom of thought,
And Thine own path, O God of virtues,
    Till I go to sleep this night.

Catherine Maclennan
from her mother, and her mother before her, and her mother before her

As another day begins

Lord Jesus, you long to come as a light into our lives. As another day begins, help us to be open to your light, that in it we may see all things clearly, and in us, those whom we meet may see you.

Elizabeth Brinkman

Thank you for the morning

Lord Jesus, thank you for the morning. Let us open our eyes and see your beauty. Today we might have bad times; there might be things that try us, some of us might have no money to pay the rent, we might have no money to heat our rooms or we might be worried about our jobs, children might be sick, but Lord, we know you understand.

So Father, this day when we wake up to all the troubles of the world and when we open a newspaper and we see all the areas of disasters, all the fighting, we remember the love of the Lord.

May that love stay in our hearts always and give us strength to bear whatever burden we have to bear. Not that we deserve all these qualities, but because you in your kindness have offered it.

Give us the humility to accept your gift and the intelligence to treasure it always. In Jesus' name, we ask this. Amen.

Dr. Swee Chai Ang

 *Send me out*

I bring you myself this day—my body, mind and spirit—in worship and praise and service. Send me out in your spirit to do your will in your world: to stand for your truth and purpose and seeking love. Let my humble offering of life contribute to your honor and glory. Amen.

Rita Snowden

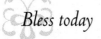 *Bless today*

O God . . .

Bless today, all my goings and comings.

Bless my home, and all who share it.

Bless my small menial tasks, and my larger plans stretching away into the future. Save me from self-importance, from self-centeredness. You have set me here with the power to share: let the spirit of Jesus Christ, your Son, be in some measure mine this day. Amen.

Rita Snowden

Help me get through today

Lord, please help me to get through today. I'm dreading this afternoon; people can be so difficult. Lord, give me patience!

Angela Ashwin

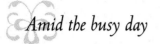 *Amid the busy day*

Open our eyes that we may see thee at work in the midst of the turmoil and tension of our day. Open our hearts that we may receive the gift of thy love, given for the whole world.

Women of Uruguay

Thanks for the little things

Thank You, God, for little things
that come unexpectedly
To brighten up a dreary day
that dawned so dismally—
Thank You, God, for sending
a happy thought my way
To blot out my depression
on a disappointing day—
Thank You, God, for brushing
the dark clouds from my mind
And leaving only sunshine
and joy of heart behind.

Helen Steiner Rice

For families, friends, and neighbors

Into your hands

Father, I place into your hands
my friends and family.
Father, I place into your hands
the things that trouble me.
Father, I place into your hands
the person I would be,
for I know I always can trust you.

Jenny Hewer
©1975 Thankyou Music, PO Box 75, Eastbourne, East Sussex,
BN23 6NW, UK. Used by permission.

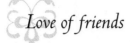 *Love of friends*

Lord, I see clearly that any affection which I have ever had is
scarcely as one drop in the vast ocean of all the seas, when
compared with the tenderness of Thy divine heart towards
those whom I love. . . . Therefore I cannot even by one thought
wish anything other than that which Thy almighty wisdom
has appointed for each of them. . . . Lord, bless Thy special
friends and mine, according to the good pleasure of Thy divine
goodness.

Saint Gertrude the Great (1256–ca. 1302) and
Saint Mechtilde (ca. 1241–ca. 1299)

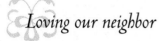Loving our neighbor

Dear Lord Jesus Christ, who commanded us to love our neighbors as ourselves, make me much more wide awake to the needs and hopes and loves of those I meet from day to day. Give me a share in your love and understanding, the love that enabled you to pierce the defenses of the outer man and to understand the longing that is deep in everyone's heart. And give me courage to speak your truth and love with my neighbor.

Susan Coupland

The joys and tensions of family life

Father of all,
we thank you for our families and friends
and for all the joys and tensions
    which are part of family life.
Give to us grace
to become more loving and more forgiving
that our homes may be places where we may grow daily
into the likeness of your Son, Jesus Christ,
to whom be praise and glory.

Women of Thailand

 *Faithful in love*

Lord, help us to be faithful in loving those you have brought into our lives. Keep us free from needless distractions so that we can give our best energies in faithful service to them and to you.

Kathy Keay

Teach us to be careful

O Father, we thank you
for the close ties which bind us
as parents, sisters, brothers, husbands, wives and children.
Teach us, good Lord, not to be careless
of those who are dearest to us.
Give us the kindness of the Master
and develop in us
a deeper, more tender and sincere love for them.

Women of Jamaica

Families of the world

O Lord Jesus, who came on earth as a child of a human family,
we bring before you the families throughout the world.
Grant that we may know how much we are dependent
    upon one another,
that we may open the doors of our homes and hearts
    for those in need,
that we may realize more fully the blessings and riches
    of the human family.

Women of Africa

Help us to listen

We pray for patience to listen to our neighbors, whether or not they listen to us.

Spirit of Christ, increase our patience.

For love towards those whom we find irritating or complaining or dull.

Spirit of Christ, enlarge our love.

For that concern which gives not only gifts, but time, for those in need.

Spirit of Christ, widen our concern.

For humility to receive graciously as well as to give generously.

Spirit of Christ, grant us humility.

Women of New Zealand

Selfless giving

I want to love like you, Lord,
letting go of my greed for glory,
   giving those I love the freedom to be themselves.
But giving up self-centeredness is harder
   than giving up life itself.
Help me to do it.

Veronica Zundel

When life is hard

A cry from the heart

Lord—why? What have I done to you
that you can do this to me?
I thought you cared, I thought you were good;
why have you turned against me?
No, don't give me textbook answers
about the why and how of suffering!
Just—please—give me some sense of being held
while the questions are wept and swept
to a stillness within.

Kate Compston

Help!

Lord, please help. I feel negative.
Everything is black.
It's dark and it's cold and it's everything it shouldn't be.
What shall I do?
Show me.

Evelyn Christenson

Loneliness

Christ,
praying in the Garden while others slept
you know the necessity
and the pain
of standing alone.
Be with me now in my loneliness.
Help me to find strength in solitariness,
peace in the silence,
and the presence of God
in the absence of friends.
Turn my thoughts from myself
that I may seek
not so much to find companionship
as to give companionship to others.

Margaret T. Taylor

On being turned back from suicide

I'm in Your hands.
You stopped me.
You must show me what to do.

Loren Hurnscot

God in all things

Lord, You fill all things.
Give us grace to look for You where You are closest at hand,
not in consecrated buildings,
but in the hearts of those with whom we do not get along.

Susan Williams

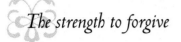

The strength to forgive

Lord, give me the strength to forgive this person.

Evelyn Christenson

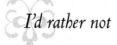

I'd rather not

Lord,
I heard your voice today.
You said something I'd rather not hear.
I prayed about that awkward person, you know,
the one that drives me mad. I reminded you
how often I've been hurt, annoyed, irritated and upset.
And you said, "Love one another as I have loved you."

Pam Weaver

Accepting suffering

Lord Jesus, help me to accept willingly whatever suffering I am called to bear in my life. Show me how to shoulder my burdens as you did—purely and simply for love, and grant me the gift of patience.

Sylvia Hunter

Deep peace

Lord, the one that I love is sick and in great pain; out of your compassion heal him and take away his pain. It breaks my heart to see him suffer; may I not share his pain if it is not your will that he be healed?

Lord, let him know that you are with him; support and help him that he may come to know you more deeply as a result of his suffering.

Lord, be our strength and support in this time of darkness and give us that deep peace which comes from trusting you.

Etta Gullick

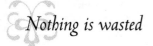

Nothing is wasted

Praise you, Redeemer, that your purpose is to restore all things.
No love, grief or work of ours is wasted when we give it to you.

Veronica Zundel

Help us to help others

Carrying out God's work

God of love, help us to remember
that Christ has no body now on earth but ours,
no hands but ours, no feet but ours.
Ours are the eyes to see the needs of the world.
Ours are the hands with which to bless everyone now.
Ours are the feet with which he is to go about doing good.

Saint Teresa of Avila (1515–1582)

How sweet it is to serve

Jesus, my suffering Lord,
grant that today and every day
I may see You in the person of Your sick ones,
and that in caring for them I may serve You.
Grant also that even in the guise of the fretful,
the demanding, the unreasonable,
I may still recognize You and say:
My suffering Jesus, how sweet it is to serve You.

Mother Teresa of Calcutta (1910–1997)

In unexpected ways

Lord Jesus Christ, . . .
you come in unexpected ways
and speak through people
whose background and outlook
are different from our own.
Help us to listen with respect
to their experience
and reflect upon their insights.
Free us from pride
to find your dignity and presence
wherever you are.

Maureen Edwards

Our neighbor's needs

Guide us that we may be more sensitive to our neighbor's needs.
We pray for awareness of those needs:
    the need of the old to know they are wanted,
    the need of the young to feel they are listened to,
    the need of all people to know they are of value.
Lord, keep us aware.

Women of New Zealand

Refreshment in weariness

Dead tired

Dead-tired Jesus,
help me and my dear ones to endure patiently
the helpless weakness of our souls and bodies.

Four Lithuanian women imprisoned in northern Siberia for their faith

I am so tired

Jesus, you said,
>"Come to me all who are weary and heavy laden
>>and I will give you rest."

I come, Lord, tired and dejected.
But I come
>knowing you will refresh me;
>knowing you will give me strength for another day;
>knowing you will surround me with your love.

I come,
>and leave my burdens at your feet.

Rosemary Atkins

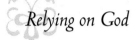
Relying on God

Not relief from pain, not relief from the weariness that follows, nor anything of that sort at all, is my chief need. Thou, O Lord God, art my need—Thy courage, Thy patience, Thy fortitude. And very much I need a quickened gratitude for the countless helps given every day.

Amy Carmichael (1868–1951)
written while ill and in pain

# No strength left

My God, I am able no more: *be able* for me!
(Je n'en peux plus: *pouvez* pour moi!)

Madame Acarie (1566–1618)

All that wearies me

To Thee I bring my care,
The care I cannot flee;
Thou wilt not only share
But bear it all for me:
O loving Savior, now to Thee
I bring the load that wearies me.

Frances Ridley Havergal (1836–1879)

Tired of giving

Lord, when we grow tired of giving,
feel frustration, hurt and strain,
by your Spirit's quiet compulsion,
draw us back to you again.
Guide us through the bitter searching
when our confidence is lost;
give us hope from desolation,
arms outstretched upon a cross.

Jill Jenkins

Asking for strength

Lord, I am tired and afraid.
Yes, Lord, I know my charge is simple:
    to love and serve you,
    to keep the faith,
    to spread your living kindness.
Lord, give me the strength
    to continue in your service.

Sybil Phoenix

The daily round

Till my work is done

God give me work
Till my life shall end
And life
Till my work is done.

Winifred Holtby (1898–1935)

 *By my side*

Father, hear the prayer I offer;
  not for ease that prayer shall be,
but for strength that I may ever
  live my life courageously.

Be my strength in hours of weakness,
  in my wanderings be my guide;
through endeavor, failure, danger,
  Father, be thou by my side.

  Love Maria Willis (1824–1908)
  altered

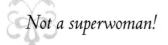

Not a superwoman!

Lord, I admit that I know I am not superwoman.
Forgive me for acting like I am.
Show me what you want me to do,
    and what you want me to lay aside.
Thank you for accepting me just as I am. Amen.

Anonymous

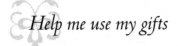 *Help me use my gifts*

Creative Father, you made me able to do, think and understand.
I want to say "I can," but often I fear failure.
Help me to accept my gifts and dedicate them to you.

Veronica Zundel

At work

 Partnership with God

Lord, in union with the love which made Thee deign to occupy Thyself in work. . . . I beg Thee to unite my work with Thy most perfect acts and make it perfect: as a drop of water, poured into a great river, does all that river does.

Lord, I desire that, at all times, those who profit by my labor may be not only refreshed in body, but may also be drawn to Thy love and strengthened in every good.

Saint Gertrude the Great (1256–ca. 1302) and
Saint Mechtilde (ca. 1241–ca. 1299)

Those without work

As we enjoy our jobs today, we would not forget
   those who have none;
   those who have no expectation of suitable work;
   those who are worried because of family needs;
   those finding their strength overtaxed;
   those waiting long for advancement and reward;
   those entering upon retirement and the loss of lifelong
      interests;
   those frail and old, and on the brink of the new life. Amen.

Rita Snowden

Working together with God

Christ the Workman, make me holy,
Christ the Savior, make me true;
Make of me a thing of beauty,
Show me how to labor too;
Fellow worker would I be
Ever, blessed Lord, with Thee.

D. Helen Stone

Setting priorities

Lord Jesus, your days were much more demanding than mine. You never had a quiet desk to sit at and compose yourself. The people clamored. You lived out of a rucksack.

Help me to recognize your priorities today—usually people and their needs. Help me live today as you want me to.

Dorothy Stewart

Authority

Christ our Lord,
you refused the way of domination
and died the death of a slave.
May we also refuse to lord it
over those who are subject to us,
but share the weight of authority
so that all may be empowered
in your name. Amen.

Janet Morley

After stepping down

Our Father, when I see someone else doing the work, holding the offices, and receiving the attention I did, help me to praise and give support. Keep me from stressing "the way *we* did" or announcing *"we* tried that and it didn't work." If my experience can be useful, help me to share it—when someone asks. In time of difficulty, may I speak the right words of encouragement. As the child playing games learns that he cannot be *it* all the time, so help me to participate unobtrusively and cheerfully.

Josephine Robertson

Marriage

On a thin wedding band

I thank thee, Father, for the meaning of this timeworn wedding ring, blessed in a sacrament many years ago. It was shiny then, even as our faces were young, unlined, glowing with hope for the future. Through this bond we have known joy and sorrow, struggle and achievement, children, a busy home—gradually grown quiet—and the delight of grandchildren. We have experienced the richness of family life and the joy of companionship. I thank thee that our marriage vows have meant so much and for the fulfillment symbolized by this thin gold band.

Josephine Robertson

When things go wrong

Lord, teach me to accept, and in accepting to see all things as part of your plan in drawing us closer to you. When things go wrong between us, let me see there may be some very good reason for it. May I see clearly my own mistakes and overcome them. Teach me to make loving and giving the center of our every day.

Rosa George

Help us to grow together

Lord, we come to you about our marriage. Help us to begin to put things right. In the quietness show us how to stop thinking of the other's faults and failures and to recognize our own.

Check our negative responses and give us a vision of the partnership that we can create anew with your help. Where we do not yet feel love, give us good intents and wishes for each other's well-being that will bring us closer. Reawaken, in time, we pray, the love we once felt for each other and make us tenderhearted and forgiving because you, in Christ, freely forgive and receive us.

Mary Batchelor

The gift of time

O Lord, we pray for those who, full of confidence and love, once chose a partner for life, and are now alone after final separation.

May they receive the gift of time, so that hurt and bitterness may be redeemed by healing and love, personal weakness by your strength, inner despair by the joy of knowing you and serving others; through Jesus Christ our Lord.

Susan Williams

Homemaking

Housework

Dear God,

    You know just how often housework gets me down.

    Please help me as I begin it today, to do it with care and patience so that I may show love for my family in a practical and useful way.

Heather Harvey

Hands

This morning, Lord,
these hands planted silver beet,
fed chooks, children, cat, sparrows,
and skimmed pips off a batch of plum jam.
This morning, like any other day,
there were beds to make, washing to be done,
and a patch sewn on the knee of a child's jeans.

This afternoon, Lord,
one of these hands got a blister from the ax handle
and the other, a splinter from kindling wood,
but the afternoon brought deeper pain
when my hands closed tight to hide anxiety
then later opened to brush away tears
before anyone could notice.
It's been a day of ups and downs
with not much quiet in between.

Now, this evening, Lord,
I come forward to receive you
and hold out these hands like a cup
for the bread of your sacred body.

And I discover
that as you bless my hands with your presence,
so you bless all their efforts.
All the planting, baking, cleaning, mending,
everything touched, everything tended,
all my fears and tears, my loving, my hurting,
the whole up-and-down day, Lord,
is suddenly Eucharist.

Joy Cowley

Unexpected visitors

They'll be here soon, the visitors I wasn't expecting and really don't want very much—but thank you for them.

Bless this house (and help me to get it cleaned up in time). This kitchen (and help me to find in it something worthy of guests).

Bless my dear foolish husband who invited them, and me as I strive to be a good hostess and a good wife to him.

Bless this table that I'm preparing; this tablecloth (thank you that it's clean); this china and silver, these candles, wobbly though they are. This room, this meal—may it all turn out to be shining and good and lovely, to compensate for my sense of distress, ill humor, of not wanting to bother.

Oh, Lord, thank you for these guests as they drive toward us (and make them drive slowly, please).

I send out my thoughts of love toward them, I send out welcome, and these thoughts ease my nervousness and make me genuinely glad inside.

Thank you for their friendship. Thank you that they have telephoned us and can come. Thank you for the greetings and the news and the ideas we will exchange.

Fill us all with rejoicing. Make us feel your presence among us. Bless our coming together in the warm hospitality of my house.

Marjorie Holmes

A shopper's prayer

Lord, help us to be the kind of customer who is a joy to serve;
to be polite, especially when we have cause to be rude; to be
patient, especially when we are kept waiting for an unreasonable
period; to explain clearly what we need, and not to blame the
salesperson if it is not available.

And as we stand in line or wait in front of counters, remind
us to pass the time of waiting with a prayer for the one who is
serving.

Beryl Bye
adapted

Children

The gift of a child

Thank you for this tiny child,
and for the privilege of parenthood.

Anonymous

A mother's prayer

What do I ask for myself, Father?
Give me confidence in my own ability;
Load me down with good, plain, old-fashioned common sense;
Let me get my priorities straight—may I never be a servant to
    my house!
I run *it,* not the reverse.
It is important that I find time to play with my children.
Help me to be patient, calm and understanding, even when I
    feel like blowing my top;
Tap me on my shoulder and remind me that these feelings will
    soon pass away, but my words may never be forgotten.
It is strange how my children reflect my moods right back at me;
if I am irritable, or happy, so are they.
I feel that it is mostly up to me to set the tone of our home.
Help me not to be self-centered.

My needs can generally wait until the children are not so
      dependent on me;
this time with them while they are so young is very precious;
it will not last long, but out of it will come many beautiful
      memories to treasure in the future.
There is so much for which I could ask, to help me to be a good
      wife and mother.
But there is one thing I desire above all; that you will show me
      how to love.
Then I believe all other things will follow.

Heather Harvey

Praying for our children

Father, hear us, we are praying,
Hear the words our hearts are saying,
We are praying for our children.

Keep them from the powers of evil,
From the secret, hidden peril,
Father, hear us for our children.

From the whirlpool that would suck them
From the treacherous quicksand, pluck them,
Father, hear us for our children.

From the worldling's hollow gladness,
From the sting of faithless sadness,
Father, Father, keep our children.

Through life's troubled waters steer them,
Through life's bitter battle cheer them,
Father, Father, be Thou near them.

Amy Carmichael (1868–1951)

Newborn child

Lord,
here she is, a real, live human being.
After all that waiting, planning, wondering,
she's finally here.
She makes my heart swell with joy.
Thank you, God, for this very special child.

Anonymous

A moment's peace

I just had to get away.

Excuse me for talking to you from the bathroom, God,
    but I've just locked myself in here.
    I need to escape for a little while from the noise and
        demands of my little children.
    Usually I can take their noise, but it's getting to me today;
        I had to leave before I exploded.

How wonderful it is to be by myself.
    Now in this precious moment I'll relax and let peace flood
        though me, removing the tension.
    Beautiful, beautiful quietness.
    Peace. Be still.

Well, they have tracked me down again and are hammering on
    the door.
   It doesn't matter, though, for I feel renewed, refreshed.
   Thank you for the miracle of silence.
   But you'd better turn up the volume on your still, small
     voice, because I'm moving back into my noisy world.

Heather Harvey

Starting school

Lord, lots of boys and girls will be off to school for the first time today—little ones, shy ones, eager ones. We remember especially [*names*]. Bless all the homes they leave, and all those who love them; all teachers who receive them—learning their names—and all friends and playmates they will meet today.

Rita Snowden
adapted

Leaving home

Father, we commit to your care our child who is leaving home. We thank you for the years of happiness and shared experience, for the laughter, tears and talking together. We thank you for every sign of your grace in his life. We commit to you the failures and disappointments too.

Now give us the humility to stand aside from his life and choices. Give us wisdom, tact and love that we may support without being intrusive and be at hand without getting in the way.

Take him into your strong keeping for your love is greater than ours.

Mary Batchelor

She's growing up

Hello God,
I'm feeling a little lost at the moment.
Not lost that I don't know where I am going,
    but just lost. Perhaps redundant may be a better word.
My teenage daughter, away from home, at college, has a
        boyfriend.
Not that I object; I'm very happy for her.
And I've met him and he genuinely seems very caring and
        considerate towards her.
But oh! I do miss the hugs, and the conversations.
I guess he's getting the hugs now.
I've told her that I miss the hugs.
I still get some, but they don't feel the same now.
I guess she is growing up and growing away,
    as she has someone else to think about.

I am pleased because she is happy.
But a little part of me feels sad.

   Still, I must pull myself together—
I've other family to think about, and care for.
So I mustn't be selfish,
just thankful—and thank you—
that she's happy.

Jane Fry

The ledgers of love

Oh, Lord, let me not dwell on the ingratitude of sons and daughters. . . . Bless them.

Let me not call up a list of their faults and failings. . . . Help them.

Deliver me from the miserable mental balance sheets that my weak and foolish nature keeps trying to make come out right.

Help me to remember that whatever most of us do for our children we do it out of instinct, duty, and our own pleasure in doing it. . . . Thank you for those things, which were their own reward.

God, bless my own parents who did so much for me, and whom I probably failed and hurt unknowingly many times. Let their kindness, common sense, and forgiveness fill me now and flow out to my sons and daughters, who cannot realize.

When they're too busy to write or phone, when they seem to me thoughtless, inconsiderate, even cruel—forgive them, bless them, and ease the strain of their lives.

Give me the gift of understanding, God. You, who must understand and forgive so much of all of us, your children, please guide me now.

Let me judge not, that I be not judged.

The accounts are closed. The ledgers of love are balanced. Thank you for this freeing knowledge, Lord.

Marjorie Holmes

For a new grandchild

Bless, I pray, this beautiful child, so newly come into our family.
I thank thee for the wonder and privilege of looking for the
first time on the tiny face of our child's child. We anticipate
his/her first smiles, first words, first steps, and pray that he/she
may flourish in a climate of affection. May we be a loving link
for him/her with an earlier generation. I pray that he/she may
grow up into a peaceful world where he/she may realize all
his/her potential, maturing from a happy childhood to a life of
accomplishment and service.

Josephine Robertson

A grandmother's prayer

Lord,
teach me to love my grandchildren as a grandmother should:
not interfering, only understanding;
not pushing myself, just being there when wanted.
Teach me to be the sort of grandmother
my children and my children's children
would want me to be.

Rosa George

Worrying about children

Lord, we give into your care our children who are causing us so much worry. The days are gone when we could correct them and tell them what to do. Now that they are grown up we have to stand by and watch them making mistakes and doing what is foolish or wrong.

Thank you that you have gone on loving and forgiving us, your wayward children, over many years. Help us to be loving and forgiving to our own children. Help us never to stop praying for them. We earnestly ask you to bring them back to yourself and to us.

Ease our own torment and distress and give us peace in trusting you, especially in the dark hours of the night. You are our heavenly Father, who loves our children more than we do and we bring them to you now, in Jesus' name.

Mary Batchelor

Our bodies

Created in God's image

O God, our loving Lord,

We give you thanks that you have created us in your image. You have given us the freedom to use our minds and bodies which you have created. It is your purpose that we take responsibility for ourselves in eating, in drinking, in the use of our time, in our work, in sexual fulfillment, and in all our relationships with others. Help us to consecrate not just our minds and spirits but our whole selves to you.

Women of Thailand

True beauty

Oh, Lord, forgive our foolishness,
    our vanity, and pride
As we strive to please the eye of man
    and not God who sees "inside."
And little do we realize
    how contented we would be
If we knew that we were beautiful
    when our hearts are touched by Thee.

Helen Steiner Rice

At home in my body

God our Father,
You chose that your Son Jesus
should be born of a woman's body.
Help me to feel at home in my body,
and to love and look after it
because you created it.

Bridget Wellard

A lump in my breast

O God, I have found a lump in my breast
and I don't want to know.
My imagination is running riot
and I'm scared. Why me, Lord?
What have I done to deserve this?
But why not me?

Forgive me, Lord, but I panicked!
You are still here
with all the love, concern and compassion
I have always claimed and relied upon.
You want for me only that which is the most loving,
so I trust you to see me through.
I'm still scared,
but with you I can face the future.

In the name of Jesus Christ,
touch me with your healing power,
that power which brings an awareness of your presence
with all its peace and serenity.

Whatever happens,
you will be with me,
giving me grace and strength to cope.
Thank you, Lord, for the faith
you have given me to rely upon you.

Rosemary Atkins

Father, bless me

Father, bless to me my body,
Father, bless to me my soul,
Father, bless to me my life,
Father, bless to me my belief.

Mary Gillies

Getting older

You never grew old

Jesus, who never grew old, it is not easy for any of us to face old age. It is fine to be young, attractive, strong. Old age reminds us of weakness and dependence upon others. But to be your disciple means accepting weakness and interdependence. Because of you we can rejoice in weakness in ourselves, and be tender to it in others.

Monica Furlong

Prayer of an aging woman

Lord, you know better than I know myself that I am growing older, and will some day be old. Keep me from getting talkative, and particularly from the fatal habit of thinking that I must say something on every subject and on every occasion.

Release me from craving to straighten out everybody's affairs. Make me thoughtful but not moody; helpful but not bossy. With my vast store of wisdom it seems a pity not to use it all, but you know, Lord, that I want a few friends at the end. Keep my mind from the recital of endless details—give me wings to come to the point.

I ask for grace enough to listen to the tales of others' pains. But seal my lips on my own aches and pains—they are increasing, and my love of rehearsing them is becoming sweeter as the years go by. Help me to endure them with patience.

I dare not ask for improved memory, but for a growing humility and a lessening of cocksureness when my memory seems to clash with the memories of others. Teach me the glorious lesson that occasionally it is possible that I may be mistaken.

Keep me reasonably sweet. I do not want to be a saint—
some of them are so hard to live with—but a sour old woman
is one of the crowning works of the devil.

Give me the ability to see good things in unexpected places,
and talents in unexpected people. And give me, O Lord, the
grace to tell them so.

A seventeenth-century nun

Menopause

God, source of all understanding,
    be with me as the changes happen in my body.
Help me to remember that
    it is a normal process for every woman.

Help me to come to terms with my changing moods.
Take away my feelings of guilt when my temper frays.
Make me seek medical advice if this is needed.

May this be a time of new assessment,
    a time to look at new horizons,
    at new opportunities,
and may I never lose sight of my part
    in your creation.

Rosemary Atkins

Death and bereavement

From birth to death

O God who brought us to birth,
and in whose arms we die,
in our grief and shock
contain and comfort us;
embrace us with your love,
give us hope in our confusion,
and grace to let go into new life,
through Jesus Christ, Amen.

Janet Morley

Give me strength

Lord God, make me strong and of good courage. All the beauty of our past life together, the home we made, the dignity and glory of it, the fellowship, the humor, the conspiracies, the discussions, the beating, fervent, keen, pulsating life; the splendid web which Thou gavest us to weave—all this is over. With one touch Thou calledst him home, and it has fallen to pieces round me. Give me strength and power to be still and see what Thou wilt do.

Mrs. Benson, wife of Edward Benson, archbishop of Canterbury
written at the time of his death

In that day

O Lord Jesus, who knowest them that are Thine;
When Thou rewardest Thy servants the prophets,
remember, we beseech Thee, for good those who have taught us,
    counseled us, guided us,
and in that day, show them mercy.
When Thou rewardest the saints,
remember, we beseech Thee, for good those who have
        surrounded us
    with holy influences,
    borne with us, forgiven us, sacrificed themselves for us,
        loved us,
and in that day, show them mercy.
Nor forget any, nor forget us,
but in that day show us mercy,
O Lord, Thou lover of souls.

Christina Rossetti (1830–1894)

At last

O my Lord! at last the longed-for hour has come!
It is now time for us to see one another!

Saint Teresa of Avila (1515–1582)
written while on her deathbed

Prayers for special occasions

Come to my heart

Thou didst leave thy throne
and thy kingly crown
when thou camest to earth for me,
but in Bethlehem's home
there was found no room
for thy holy nativity:
O come to my heart, Lord Jesus!
There is room in my heart for thee.

Emily E. S. Elliott (1836–1897)

Thank you

Thank you,
scandalous God,
for giving yourself to the world
not in the powerful and extraordinary
but in weakness and the familiar:
in a baby; in bread and wine.

Thank you
for offering, at journey's end, a new beginning;
for setting, in the poverty of a stable,
the richest jewel of your love;
for revealing, in a particular place,
your light for all nations. . . .

Thank you
for bringing us to Bethlehem, House of Bread,
where the empty are filled,
where the filled are emptied;
where the poor find riches,
and the rich recognize their poverty;
where all who kneel and hold out their hands
are unstintingly fed.

Kate Compston

New Year

Guide us through this year

Almighty One,
who brought us through the darkness of sleep
    to the bright light of this new day,
guide us through this year:
    in dark and light,
    in pain and joy,
    in snow and sun,
    through heartbreak to Sonbright,
and from today's joyous light
bring us to the guiding light of eternity.

Kate McIlhagga

GOOD FRIDAY

Watching by the cross

Christ, whose bitter agony
was watched from afar by women,
enable us to follow the example
of their persistent love;
that, being steadfast in the face of horror,
we may also know the place of resurrection,
in your name, Amen.

Janet Morley

EASTER

Free me

Lord God,
my Maker and Master,
help me to be free this Easter:
free from my past sin and present despair,
free to follow Christ as your obedient servant.

Jenny Petersen

The fragrance of love

Flower fragrance of anointed love,
fill our house, our hearts, our world,
with the life-giving news of Easter.

Kate McIlhagga

Roll back the stone

When we are all despairing;
when the world is full of grief;
when we see no way ahead,
and hope has gone away:
Roll back the stone.

Although we fear change;
although we are not ready;
although we'd rather weep
and run away:
Roll back the stone.

Because we're coming with the women;
because we hope where hope is vain;
because you call us from the grave
and show the way:
Roll back the stone.

Janet Morley

Renewal and resurrection

My Lord, my Master, my Friend whose never-failing love conquered sin and death, I love you and adore you. I bless you for the renewal and resurrection of this lovely spring day. I ask that the love from which your resurrection sprang may awaken my heart to love you more dearly and follow you more nearly.

Susan Coupland

Walk with us, Lord

Lord, when we walk away from our problems, meet us on the road; when we are dejected and alone, bring us the joy of Your companionship, that we may carry the power of resurrection into a dead and despairing world.

Susan Williams

A CHILD IS BORN

Prayer for a new baby

The blessing of the Holy Three,
Little love, be dower to thee,
Wisdom, Peace and Purity.

> *Esther de Waal*
> *echoing the* Carmina Gadelica

Thanksgiving at a baptism

We praise you, Lord, for Jesus Christ,
who died and rose again;
he lives to break the power of sin
and over death to reign.

We praise you, Lord, for Jesus Christ,
he loves this child we bring;
he frees, forgives, and heals us all,
he lives and reigns as King.

We praise you that this child now shares
the freedom Christ can give,
has died to sin with Christ, and now
with Christ is raised to live.

Judith B. O'Neill

PART THREE

The Wider World

We are closely linked to our sisters around the world,
and we care about the world outside our front doors
and offices.
Here are prayers for our world—

> *for peace and justice,*
> *for the homeless and for refugees,*
> *for the damaged and the unloved,*
> *for the underpaid and the unemployed,*
> *for the elderly and for children,*
> *for the environment and our concerns about*
>> *pollution and materialism.*

Many of these prayers were written by groups of women
for the annual Women's World Day of Prayer services.
They can be prayed at home alone just as well as in a
group or congregational setting.

Teach us to care

Show us, Lord

Lord,
show us where there is loneliness,
   . . . that we may take friendship.
Show us where individuals are not seen as persons,
   . . . that we may acknowledge their identity.
Show us where there is alienation,
   . . . that we may take reconciliation.

Women of Jamaica

Bearing thy love to others

Help me to love the world
  as Thou dost love it
and for Thy sake and its sake
  to forego all things that hinder me
  in bearing Thy love to others.

Marjorie Milne (1907–1977)

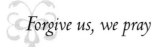

Forgive us, we pray

Lord,
we confess that we have been arrogant and self-indulgent,
  making human power absolute,
  ever seeking to satisfy our never-ending desires.
Have mercy on us.

We have despised one another,
  acting with cruelty, prejudice, suspicion and jealousy.
Soften our unrepentant hearts that will not accept other people.
Forgive our sins, we pray.

We have been weak in the face of the evils of this world.
We have been indifferent, as though we shared no responsibility
  for the sin and the suffering of the rest of the world.
Forgive us, we pray.

Women of Japan

Teach us to care

Lord, teach us to care,
Give it to us to see beyond the gray street, or the green
      countryside,
  or the sparkle of the sea, or the glory of the mountains.
Give it to us to love, as Thou dost love all the nations of
      the world.
Give it to us to give as Thou didst give, holding nothing back.

Amy Carmichael (1868–1951)

I have cut myself off from you

Lord,

I am afraid to admit that others suffer through my lack of
    self-giving.

I refuse to hear the cries of the hungry, the unloved, the hurt,
    the lonely, the despairing.

I know that as long as I choose isolation, true community
    cannot be.

I am unwilling to give up my comforts and pleasures that others
    may have a better life.

Lord, in failing to see my responsibility to others, I have cut
    myself off from you.

Forgive me, Lord, where I fail you and others.

Women of Canada

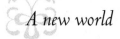
A new world

Give us, Father, a vision of your world as love would make it:
a world whose benefits are shared, so that everyone can
enjoy them;
a world whose different people and cultures live with
tolerance and mutual respect;
a world where peace is built with justice, and justice is fired
with love;
and give us the courage to build it, through Jesus Christ
our Lord.

Women of Guatemala

Hear us, Lord

Lord, we pray
—for all who suffer, for any reason:
   grant them comfort and strength.
—for all who make moral and political decisions:
   grant them wisdom and humility.
—for those who work for peace, justice and the good of all
      humanity:
   assure them of your enabling power.
—for your Church in all the world:
   may its compassion be a true expression of your love
      revealed to us in Jesus Christ our Lord.

Women's World Day of Prayer
International Executive Committee

Where can we find peace?

O God, Father of our Lord Jesus Christ,
    the Prince of Peace:
We seek Your guidance in a world trembling with fear
    at the destructiveness of evil.
The world that You created and that You love is drenched
    with the blood of war and torn by dissension and conflict.
We, who should love each other, hate each other,
We envy each other, we harm each other,
Where can we find peace in the world?
Lord, hear the voices of those wounded in body, mind and spirit
    which rise from all corners of the earth.

Women of Japan

Give us understanding

May the Spirit of God come upon us, so that
   having eyes, we are able to see what is happening in the
      world today;
   having ears, we are able to hear the voices that clamor
      and the cries that go up from every continent,
      seeking peace, justice, liberation;
   and be educated by our experience and understanding.

Women of Mexico

Our father, your children

World citizens

We thank you, Lord, that we are citizens of a world made up of different races. Your grace touches us all whatever our race or color. We rejoice in the richness of our cultures, our music and dance, our folklore and legends. We thank you for all these gifts. We delight in the joy they bring to our lives.

Women of Brazil

Christ is in all

For our failure to realize that the whole world is a family, that
there cannot be Greek and Jew, but Christ is all and in all:

O Lord, forgive.

For our prejudice and self-consciousness of race or color or
tongue:

O Lord, forgive.

For our indifference and lack of concern for our fellows living
in poverty and unemployment and for children who are under-
nourished, ill-clothed, ill-housed, illiterate and ill:

O Lord, forgive.

For our unwillingness to understand the needs and problems of
other peoples, the bitterness of the weak, and the groans of the
oppressed:

O Lord, forgive.

For our readiness to acquiesce in the ways of the majority, to seek
the path of least resistance and to prefer popularity to fairness:

O Lord, forgive.

Mrs. Rathie Selvaratnam

The Lord's prayer

Our Father in Heaven: Abba, Father, we come as your children. Your majesty and love has been shown to us through Jesus Christ. We praise and adore you that millions of people in all walks of life, in every corner of the earth, can call you Father. You are the great creator, and yet you are the caring, watchful Father found close to all humanity. God, when we call you Father, remind us that at the same time we are calling one another brother and sister.

Hallowed be your name: Father, make your name holy in our minds and hearts. Teach us that special reverence and love which only you deserve.

Your kingdom come, your will be done on earth as in heaven: God, when we pray "your kingdom come," we are cooperating with you in your desire to rule in the hearts of all people. To find and do your will may bring opposition. Lord, we feel the need to stop and sense the security of your eternal kingdom, whose values never change. Make us open to your will that your kingdom may come on earth.

Give us this day our daily bread: All good gifts of the earth come from your generous hands. Yet this abundance is not equally shared among us. While some are satisfied, others are starving.

We know that, one day, we who have plenty will be called to give account of how we have cared for those in need. Give us this day our daily bread.

And forgive us our sins as we forgive those who have sinned against us: Lord, we have done wrong. Through your mercy, we are invited to receive your forgiveness, and to overcome the hardness of our hearts. In that spirit we are able then to forgive the injustices and hurts we receive from others. Forgive us our sins as we forgive those who have sinned against us.

Lead us not into temptation, but deliver us from evil: We know the pressure of personal temptation, the pressure to take the easy way, to take the dishonest shortcut, to follow the crowd. Lord, we need deliverance from evil in our own situations.

God of life, power and love, strengthen us in resolve to do your will and to abide in goodness, whatever the cost.

Women of Burma

Our Father's children

Our Father, God, Creator of all your different children,
   teach us to love what you have created. . . .
Teach us to see people one by one
   and to acknowledge them as our Father's children,
   our brothers and sisters:
not to pigeonhole them;
   not to hammer them into unnatural molds of our own
      making,
but to rejoice in our differences,
   accepting people as they are
   —different but of equal worth—
   each one a part of God's creation,
   showing something of his love and glory.

Sybil Phoenix

And now, the headlines . . .

We pray for the places
   so often in the news
that we may not become numbed
   to the hurt of their people,
baffled by the complexity
   of their problems,
and forget that Christ
   is not the name of a faction
   but suffers with all humanity.

Jan S. Pickard

For the nations

Let us pray for the rulers and leaders of the nations,
that they may be guided aright in seeking and working
for the things that belong to peace and achieve a family of
    nations;
For the guidance and blessing
of the various Commissions of the United Nations
which are concerned with poverty, hunger, illiteracy and
    human rights;
That the nations may become neighbors
and learn to bear one another's burdens.

Mrs. Rathie Selvaratnam

Give us hope and courage

God of all races, deliver us from prejudice, greed and pride
which deny fullness of life to our neighbors.
Be with all victims of racial prejudice
and with those who are driven from their land
and whose way of life is destroyed.
Give us all hope and courage
as we seek the good of your people everywhere.

Women of Brazil

For people in need

Make us worthy

Make us worthy, Lord, to serve our fellows through the world
who live and die in poverty and hunger. Give them, through our
hands, this day their daily bread, and, by our understanding,
love, peace and joy.

Mother Teresa of Calcutta (1910–1997)

Open our hearts

Lord, open our eyes,
    that we may see you in our brothers and sisters;
Lord, open our ears,
    that we may hear the cries from the hungry, the cold, the
        frightened, the oppressed.
Lord, open our hands,
    that we may reach out to all who are in need;
Lord, open our hearts,
    that we may love each other as you love us.

Women of Canada

For the troubles of the world

We pray for those in the world who have forgotten that all people are made in your image and likeness and are of equal worth in your eyes;

> for those who suffer because of racial oppression and social injustice;
> for those who struggle for human dignity;
> for those who have lost their hope for the future.

We pray for the needy and suffering in the world;

> for the hungry and thirsty;
> for the homeless;
> for the unemployed and the unemployable;
> for the victims of alcoholism;
> for the victims of drug addiction;
> for the sick, in mind or body;
> for the lonely and the elderly.

We pray for all parents, that they may give their children the love and guidance which will help them to find the right way in life;

for all children without parents;

for young people, that they may find hope for the future;

for peace between nations and goodwill among all people;

Lord, hear us!

Women of Sweden

We bring them to you

God of the heights and the depths,
we bring to you
    those driven into the desert,
    those struggling with difficult decisions.
May they choose life.

God of the light and the darkness,
we bring to you
    those lost in the mist of drugs or drink,
    those dazzled by the use of power.
May they choose life.

God of the wild beast and the ministering angel,
we bring to you
    those savaged by others' greed,
    those exhausted by caring for others.
May they feel your healing touch.

Kate McIlhagga

For those in need

Jesus, you taught us how to pray and how to ask that we may receive. We come to you now, concerned not for ourselves, but for others. . . .

In your name we ask for blessing and mercy on all the homeless. We pray especially for those who have lost their homes through war, and who have to begin life all over again in a different and often frightening environment. We remember those who have become refugees and boat people and those who face deportation.

In your name we ask a blessing on all unemployed, underemployed and unemployable people all over the world, and on those who work in subhuman conditions.

In your name we ask for special grace for the aged, whether rich or poor, in cities or in villages, in countries large or small. Wherever people live, there are those who sit in the despondency of neglected old age. Help us to have compassion on them.

Women of the Caribbean

May we bring hope

As we pray—
>   for those for whom life has no meaning or purpose,
>   for those who are without work and those who are
>   overworked,
>   for those who are lonely or lost, in the big cities or in
>   strange lands,
>   for those who are dismayed that their efforts bring so
>   little change,

Give us courage so to act and so to speak that hope may
abound.

Women's World Day of Prayer
International Executive Committee

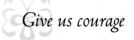 # Give us courage

Blessed Lord, you who know each one of our fears, release us
from them all by your love and give us courage to act:
  —against rejection,
    and for your love,
  —against oppression,
    and for justice,
  —against poverty,
    and for life abundant,
  —against sickness,
    and for wholeness,
  —against loneliness,
    and for companionship,
  —against violence,
    and for peace,
  —against death,
    and for life.

Women of Brazil

For the children of the world

May children no longer suffer

We pray for parents and children. We remember those who experience hunger and disease, cruelty and abuse, poverty and despair. We pray for those who, despite all their efforts and work, must watch their children suffer. We pray that all people will have the opportunities they need to learn the skills which will enable them to change the painful circumstances of their lives. In Jesus' name we pray.

Women of Burma

A child's prayer

Holy Father, we pray for the people in other lands,
especially for the boys and girls.

   Some would learn but have no teacher;

   Some are sick and have no doctor;

   Some are sad and have no one to comfort them;

   Some are hungry and poor and have no helper;

   Some are happy and cared for as we are ourselves.

For all we ask your loving care.

Supply their needs and comfort their hearts,

   through Jesus Christ our Lord.

Nancy Martin

Help us care for our children

The world's children need our prayer and concern. They are the innocent victims of war, power struggles and aggression. Many are stateless, rootless, and unwanted. Others are victims of broken families—confused and missing the security and shelter of a loving home; and often without the stability which only faith in God can give. We pray that, beginning in our homes, we may not make them victims either of affluence and indulgence, or of neglect and lack of love.

We pray for young people growing up in today's world:
- —for the bewildered and seeking, that they may find faith in You,
- —for the unemployed and frustrated, that they may find spheres of usefulness and satisfaction,
- —for those who have been led into paths of anarchy and violence, that they may find a way of escape.

May our discipline be wise and just. May our love make it easier for them to understand the love of God.

Women of Ireland

For justice and peace

Teach us your justice

Jesus Christ, teach us your new justice and unite us into one.
Holy Spirit, touch the hearts of those who *have* power.
Let them realize the greatness of the responsibility
    they have taken upon themselves
And lead them to set right the broken relationships
Between people and nations.
May they turn all their strength and ability
Towards creating a better world
Which provides sufficiently for all people on earth.

Women of Czechoslovakia

We grieve over our world

Lord, You are a God who keeps Your promises.
We grieve over our world at this time,
because people have forgotten You
    and gone their own ways.
Please scatter the proud with all their plans,
bring down the cruel and greedy rulers,
and help those who are guided by Your Spirit
    to bring peace and order.

Beryl Bye

For refugees

Lord Jesus, who as a child didst flee with Thy family to a strange country, look with pity we beseech Thee upon the refugees scattered throughout the world, victims of war and persecution, tyranny and oppression. Save them from despair, heal their bitterness, give them hope. And as they have suffered at the hands of their fellow men, so may we, their fellow men, never forget their needs; and may the causes for their homeless-ness be rooted out of our world.

Henderika J. Rynbergen

Poverty

We pray:

—for forgiveness because many are living ignorant of the
      poverty and need that exists in the world today.

—for those who believe that the poor are poor because they are
      lazy and won't work.

—for the rich who don't feel the necessity of sharing with
      the poor.

—that the poor may have the assurance that this is not God's
      will for them.

—that our education, especially in the church, will change
      these ideas.

—that the poor may not live in apathy without seeking a more
      just life.

—that the poor may not have a feeling of powerlessness as the
      dispossessed of the earth, unable to determine their own
      life and destiny.

Women of Mexico

Open our eyes

Open our eyes, O Lord, to the needs of our brothers and sisters who lack the basic necessities of life. We pray for the millions throughout the world who work for very low wages, and for those who have lost their land and their livelihood.

Make us aware of the homeless on our streets and of families without adequate shelter. Give us wisdom to deal with the causes of these problems, that all may work together for better living conditions.

Women of Brazil

Lord, you placed me here

Lord, you placed me in the world
    to be its salt.
I was afraid of committing myself,
    afraid of being stained by the world.
I did not want to hear what "they" might say.
And my salt dissolved as if in water.
Forgive me, Jesus.

Lord, you placed me in the world
    to be its light.
I was afraid of the shadows,
    afraid of the poverty.
I did not want to know other people.
And my light slowly faded away.
Forgive me, Jesus.

Lord, you placed me in the world
    to live in community.
Thus you taught me to love,
    to share in life,
    to struggle for bread and for justice,
    your truth incarnate in my life.
So be it, Jesus.

Peggy M. de Cuehlo

Searching of spirit

O Lord, Who lovest the stranger, defend and nourish, we entreat Thee, all sojourners in strange lands, and poor helpless persons, that they may glorify Thee out of grateful hearts; and to such men as are tyrannical and oppressive give searching of spirit and amendment of ways that Thou mayest show mercy on them also.

Christina Rossetti (1830–1894)

Your kingdom come—through us

When we stand gazing upwards,
bring us down to earth:
    with the love of a friend
    through the songs of the sorrowing
    in the faces of the hungry.

When we look to you for action,
demand some work from us:
    by your touch of fire
    your glare of reproof
    your fearful longing.

As ruler over all:
    love us into action;
    fire us with your zeal;
    enrich us with your grace
to make us willing subjects of your rule.

Janet Nightingale

Touch our world

God of freedom, God of justice,
God whose love is strong as death,
God who saw the dark of prison,
God who knew the price of faith:
touch our world of sad oppression
with your Spirit's healing breath.

Shirley Erena Murray
written in 1981 for Amnesty International. Text © 1992 by Hope Publishing
Co., Carol Stream, IL 60188. All rights reserved. Used by permission.

Where are you in the time of our troubles?

How can we believe in you, God, when we have to live in
   uncertainty?
How can we trust you when we can see the smoke
   rising from the volcano?
Women worry for the future of their children,
   men anguish over the harvests which may not be.
Children cling to their parents for fear of the dark.
Where is your saving hand, O God?
Where is your kindness and pity?
When hardship and fear abound, you are there in those
   who listen and take the strain.
Sharing and hospitality, self-denial and benevolence
   are the signs of your presence.
These will always be with us when you are with us,
   these will always remain as long as your love remains.
Where are you, God, in the time of our troubles?
You are always with us in the good times and the bad.
You are always with us.

   Janice Clark

For creation

Glorious creator

My God, I thank thee, who hast made
  the earth so bright;
so full of splendor and of joy,
  of grace and light;
so many glorious things are here,
of truth and right.

Adelaide A. Procter (1825–1864)

You make us glad

Thank you for people who laugh for tomorrow,
because they are glad to have life for today.
Thank you for putting us into such a wonderful world
where there is so much to make us glad.

Helen Richards

We mourn the death of forests

Lord Jesus Christ,
    through whom and for whom
    the whole universe was created,
we mourn with you the death of forests,
    fruitful lands that have become deserts,
    wild animals left without grass,
    plants, insects, birds and animals
    threatened with extinction,
    lands ravaged by war,
    people left homeless.
As the earth cries out for liberation,
    we confess our part in bringing it
    towards the brink of catastrophe.
Through ignorance,
    but often willfully,
    we thought we could serve God and mammon,
    unable to resist the temptation
    to spend and acquire more and more possessions,
    with little thought of the consequences for future generations.

Savior of the world, you call us to repentance:
    to be transformed by your love,
    deny ourselves,
    take up the cross and follow in your way.

Maureen Edwards

A prayer for the animals

O Lord, help me to be kind to all creatures.

Margaret Tottle

Action called for

Dear Father God, motivate us to take action whenever and wherever we find the creatures you created suffering from cruelty, neglect or indifference at the hands of man, woman or child, and convict us when we shy away from personal involvement.

Beryl Bye

Help us to count the cost

Father, in your creation you have made us rich,
And yet we have made ourselves poor
In our reluctance to credit others with value;
In our failure to look beyond the material and accepted
     standards of our day;
In our deafness to hear only the sounds that are pleasant to
     our ears;
In our noise and business, failing to listen
  to the unuttered cries of hurt and pain;
In our lifestyle, putting the pleasure of palate
  before the real cost to individuals in another part of
     the world.

We live as though our well-being matters most
And because of that, the rest of creation suffers.
Father, forgive us.
Help us to visualize your values,
To appreciate your resources,
But above all to credit all humankind as members of the family,
Valuable and indispensable.

Rosemary Wass

About the Contributors

Well over a hundred women contributed prayers included in this volume—contemporary women and women who lived hundreds of years ago; women from North and South America, Europe, Africa, Asia, and Australia; Catholic, Protestant, and Orthodox women; homemakers and doctors of the Church. Here is more information about some of them.

Madame Acarie (1566–1618). Wife, mother of six, and mystic, Barbe Jeanne Avrillot Acarie helped introduce the Reformed Carmelites into France. After her husband's death in 1613, she became a lay sister under the name of Marie de l'Incarnation.

Anne Brontë (1820–1849). The younger sister of Charlotte and Emily Brontë, Anne wrote *The Tenant of Wildfell Hall* and *Agnes Grey* as well as a number of poems.

Amy Carmichael (1868–1951). A Protestant missionary from Britain to India, Miss Carmichael wrote many devotional books and poems.

Saint Catherine of Genoa (1447–1510). A married woman from a noble Ligurian family, Caterina experienced mystical visions, cared for the sick, and wrote several books.

Evelyn Christenson. A pastor's wife, Evelyn Christenson is the author of many books on prayer, including the best-selling *What Happens When Women Pray.*

Esther de Waal. Author, lecturer, and retreat leader, Esther de Waal is a student of Benedictine and Celtic monasticism. Her numerous books include *The Celtic Way of Prayer: The Recovery of the Religious Imagination.*

Emily Dickinson (1830–1886). A poet who withdrew from all social contacts at the age of twenty-three, retiring to her family home in Amherst, Massachusetts, Emily Dickinson wrote nearly eighteen hundred poems, most of which were discovered and published after her death.

Madame Elizabeth of France (1764–1794). Sister of Louis XVI, Elizabeth of France died at the guillotine during the French Revolution.

Elizabeth Fry (1780–1845). An English Quaker, Elizabeth Fry visited Newgate Prison for women in 1813, was appalled by the conditions there, and devoted the rest of her life to prison and asylum reform.

Monica Furlong. *Visions and Longings: Medieval Women Mystics* is just one of Ms. Furlong's books, which include other biographies and mythic novels.

Saint Gertrude the Great (1256–ca. 1302). A contemplative following a conversion experience at age twenty-five, Saint Gertrude wrote a collection of prayers, *Exercitia Spiritualia,* and a major work in Christian mysticism, *Legatus Divinae Pietatis.*

Mary Gillies and **Catherine Maclennan.** Gillies and Maclennan are among the contributors to the *Carmina Gadelica,* a six-volume collection of traditional prayers from the Western Isles of Scotland from the 1870s onward.

Lady Jane Grey (1537–1554). Uncrowned queen of England for ten days in 1553, Lady Jane was beheaded on Tower Hill a year later at the age of seventeen.

Frances Ridley Havergal (1836–1879). Gifted in the classics and Hebrew, Frances Ridley Havergal's main interest, after her conversion to Christianity at the age of fifteen, was writing poems and hymns.

Marjorie Holmes. The author of inspirational books, novels, and magazine articles, Marjorie Holmes wrote *I've Got to Talk To Somebody, God: A Woman's Conversations with God.*

Winifred Holtby (1898–1935). A native of Yorkshire, England, Winifred Holtby was a feminist and novelist best known for her book *South Riding.*

Julian of Norwich (1342–ca. 1416). An anonymous mystic who lived as an anchoress in a cell attached to St. Julian's Church, Norwich, England, the woman who came to be known as Julian wrote about a revelation she received in 1373 of God's great love.

Elisabeth Leseur (1866–1914). A wealthy Frenchwoman, Mme. Leseur kept a diary revealing her Christian convictions. After her death, her husband read her diary and was converted. It has been published as *My Spirit Rejoices: The Diary of a Christian Soul in an Age of Unbelief.*

Mary, Queen of Scots (1542–1587). A queen when a week old, Mary was executed by order of her cousin, Queen Elizabeth I, to whom she had fled for protection.

Saint Mechtild of Magdeburg (ca. 1207–ca. 1292). Mystic and nun at the convent of Helfta, Mechtild described her religious experience in *Flowering Light of the Divinity.*

Saint Mechtilde (ca. 1241–ca. 1299). Mystic, nun, and mentor to Saint Gertrude the Great, a younger nun at the convent of Helfta. Mechtilde recorded her revelations from God, and after her death Gertrude published them in *The Book of Special Grace.*

Helen Steiner Rice. An oft-quoted Christian author, Helen Steiner Rice has written many books of devotional verses.

Christina Rossetti (1830–1894). Younger sister of the painter Dante Gabriel Rossetti, Christina expressed her Christian faith in books and poems, including the carol "In the Bleak Midwinter."

Dorothy Stewart. A writer and editor in England, Dorothy Stewart compiled this anthology. She began researching prayers by women when she realized how poorly represented women are in most published collections of prayers.

Corrie ten Boom (1892–1983). With her Dutch father and family, Corrie ten Boom hid Jews from the Nazis during the Second World War and, with her father and sister, was sent to Ravensbruck concentration camp. She is the author of several books, including *The Hiding Place.*

Saint Teresa of Avila (1515–1582). Teresa was born a Spanish noblewoman. At the age of twenty she became a nun and, after a deep experience of God, was transformed. She founded an order of Carmelite nuns and combined mysticism with a practical life of reform. In 1970 she was declared a doctor of the Church.

Mother Teresa of Calcutta (1910–1997). The founder of the Missionaries of Charity, who care for lepers, orphans, and the dying, Mother Teresa was awarded the Nobel Peace Prize in 1979 for her work.

Women's World Day of Prayer. Many prayers in this collection come from this worldwide movement of Christian women who come together to observe a common day of prayer each year on the first Friday in March. Women of a different country each year are chosen to write the service, which is translated into over a thousand languages. The day begins as morning comes first over the islands of Tonga in the South Pacific, and prayers continue round the clock around the world until the last service takes place on St. Lawrence Island off the coast of Alaska. The Women's World Day of Prayer is the largest ecumenical movement in the world organized and led by women.

Index of Authors

Index of Subjects

Faith

O God our Father, may we have, 59
Lord, forgive me for all the times, 95

Family life (see also Children; Marriage)

Father of all, we thank you, 118
O Father, we thank you for the close, 120
O Lord Jesus, who came on earth, 121

Following God

I desire one thing only, 84
Lord, tell me what you want me to do, 85
O God, I want only Your will in my life, 86
O Lord God, give me grace, 88
Lord, who forgives, give me clear sight, 91
Lord, I want you to steer, 94

Forgiveness

Lord, I know there are no limits, 28
Lord, we're sorry that we sometimes, 30
We fail You when we should hope, 34
"Forgive our sins as we forgive," 37
Lord, you know the searchings, 38
Lord, we confess that we have failed, 40
O God we ask one favor, 46
Almighty God, who knows all our dark, 80
Lord, give me the strength, 129
Lord, we confess, 213

Freedom in God

O Lord my God, I hope in Thee, 79

Love (God's love for us)
Lord, you invite us, 11
Lord, you are my lover, 50
Lord, let your love search me, 74

Loving one another
Lord, I heard your voice today, 130
Lord Jesus Christ, . . . you come, 136
Help me to love the world, 212

Marriage
I thank thee, Father, for the meaning, 155
Lord, teach me to accept, 156
Lord, we come to you, 157

Menopause
God, source of all understanding, 190

Morning
Bless to me, O God, 107
Lord Jesus, thank you for the morning, 109

Natural world
My God, I thank thee, who hast made, 250
Lord Jesus Christ, through whom, 252–53
O Lord, help me to be kind, 254
Dear Father God, motivate us, 255
Father, in your creation, 256–57

Needy
Make us worthy, Lord, to serve, 228
Lord, open our eyes, that we may, 229
We pray for those in the world, 230–31

Power of God
Holy Spirit, mighty wind of God, 26
Eternal God, you are the power, 47
You are the King of Glory, 52

Prayer, learning
O teach me to pray, Lord, 3
Lord of the field, 5
O lead us on—weigh not our merits, 39

Prayer, private
Lord, give me the joy, 15

Prayer, too distracted for
Father, forgive us that we are often, 14

Prayer, unspoken
O Lord, my heart is all a prayer, 13

Priorities
Lord Jesus, your days, 152

Racial harmony
We thank you, Lord, that we, 220
For our failure to realize, 221
God of all races, deliver us, 227

Refugees
Lord Jesus, who as a child, 241
O Lord, Who lovest the stranger, 246

Respect for each other
Our Father, God, Creator of all, 224

Stepping down from a job
Our Father, when I see someone else, 154

Strength from God
Mother me, my Father, 7
Spirit of purity and grace, 19
I need Thee every hour, 22
Merciful God, be Thou now, 64
Strength of my heart, I need not fail, 65
Lord, it seems that what I had is gone, 66
Father, hear the prayer I offer, 146

Suffering
Lord Jesus, help me to accept, 131
Lord, the one that I love is sick, 132
Not relief from pain, 140

Suicide, turned back from
I'm in Your hands, 127

Temptation
O God, our very humanity, 96

Testing times
Lord—why? What have I done to you, 124
Lord, please help. I feel negative, 125

Thanking God
You are God, 20
Thank you, Lord, for loving me, 29
We thank you, God because you give, 48–49
Lord and Master of my life, 51
We thank you, God, 53

Thank you, God, for little things, 114
Thank you for people who laugh, 251

Transformed by God
O Wind of God, come, bend us, break, 35
O God, you claim me as your partner, 75
Lord, I am a stumbling beginner, 76
Lord, let the glow of Thy great love, 77
O great Chief, light a candle within, 78
Almighty God, who knows all, 80
Lord Jesus, Rabbi, Teacher, 81
Let me not be wasted, Lord, 87

Trusting God
Thank you, Lord, that beneath, 54
Lord, guide. I know you're in charge, 55
This endless list, 57
Help me let go of trying, 58
I do not know, O God, 61
I love you, God, I trust you, 63
Lord, we know our own names, 71
Father, I place into your hands, 115

Weakness
I feel that I am weak, 45

Weariness
Dead-tired Jesus, 138
Jesus, you said, "Come to me," 139
My God, I am able no more, 141
Lord, I am tired and afraid, 144

Index of First Lines

Great and Merciful God, as the trees of the forest grow straight and tall, 12

Guide us that we may be more sensitive to our neighbor's needs, 137

Heavenly Father, we thank you, 36

Hello God, I'm feeling a little lost at the moment, 174–75

Help me let go of trying, 58

Help me to love the world, 212

Here I am, Lord—inquiring of you, 69

Here I am, O Lord, in search of myself, 25

Holy Father, we pray for the people in other lands, 237

Holy Spirit, mighty wind of God, 26

How can we believe in you, God, when we have to live in uncertainty, 249

I bring you myself this day, 110

I desire one thing only, 84

I do earnestly entreat Thee, 90

I do not know, O God, what may happen to me today, 61

I feel that I am weak, 45

I just had to get away, 170

I love you, God, 63

I need Thee every hour, most gracious Lord, 22

I thank thee, Father, for the meaning of this timeworn wedding ring, 155

I want to love like you, Lord, 123

I'm in Your hands, 127

Jesus Christ, teach us your new justice, 239

Jesus, Lord, you come to us, 16

Jesus, my suffering Lord, 135

Jesus, who never grew old, 187

Acknowledgments

We would like to thank all those who have given us permission to include prayers in this book, as indicated in the list below. Every effort has been made to trace and contact copyright owners. If there are any inadvertent omissions or errors in the acknowledgments, we apologize to those concerned and will remedy these in the next edition. All prayers except those otherwise acknowledged in the main text or listed below have been written by Dorothy Stewart. Each figure refers to the page number of the prayer.

Mary Batchelor: 157, 173, 180.

BBC Books: from *Prayer for the Day,* Hope Sealy, 108.

Catholic Supplies (N.Z.) Limited, Wellington, New Zealand: from *Aotearoa Psalms,* Joy Cowley, 160–61.

Christian Aid/SPCK: from *Bread of Tomorrow,* Janet Morley, 75, 202.

Christian Conference of Asia Youth: from *Your Will be Done,* Peggy M. de Cuehlo, 244–45.

Quoted from *Amy Carmichael of Dohnavur,* Frank Houghton (pages 164 and 334). Published by Christian Literature Crusade and used by permission: 39, 51, 77, 140. Quoted from *Gold Cord,* Amy Carmichael (pages 54, 139, 142, 156, 322, 368). Published by Christian Literature Crusade and used by permission: 5, 13, 17, 65, 93.

Church News Service: Pam Weaver, 130.

Collins Fount, an imprint of HarperCollins Publishers Limited: from *Linked in Prayer,* 57, 139, 184–85, Rosemary Atkins and others, from *Joined in Love,* 190, Rosemary Atkins and others, from *Prayers for the Family,* Rita Snowden, 111, 150, 172, from *The Love of Christ,* Mother Teresa, 88, 92, 135, from *Mother Teresa: her People and her Work,* Desmond Doig, 63, 228.

Kate Compston: from *All the Glorious Names, the Prayer Handbook 1989,* 10, from *Encounters, the Prayer Handbook 1988,* 14, 81, 82–83, 124 (both published by the United Reformed Church), from *Bread of Tomorrow,* ed. Janet Morley, published by Christian Aid/SPCK, 196–97.

Darton, Longman and Todd: from *Give Me a Hand Lord,* Heather Harvey, 159, 166–67, 170, from *Midwinter Spring,* Susan Coupland, 4, 117, 203. From *Beguine Spirituality,* Fiona Bowie (ed.), translations by Oliver Davies, © 1989. Published by SPCK: 8, 50.

Jane Fry: 174–75.

Monica Furlong: from *Prayers for Modern Man* by Monica Furlong and Helen Milton, Forward Movement Publications, 1971, 187.

Jenny Hewer: 115, copyright © Thankyou Music, PO Box 75, Eastbourne, East Sussex, BN23 6NW.

Hodder and Stoughton Limited: from *I've Got to Talk to Somebody God,* Marjorie Holmes, 162–63, 176–77.

Hope Publishing Company: from *Rejoice and Sing,* Shirley Erena Murray, 248.

© Jill Jenkins: 143.

Jean Lamb: 87.

Lutterworth Press: from *Hear a Minute,* Beryl Bye, 44, 59, 70, 80, 240, from *Prayers for all Seasons,* Beryl Bye, 99, 164, 255.

From *Heaven in Ordinary* by Angela Ashwin: 112, from *Family Book of Prayer,* Tony Castle: 156, 179, from Etta Gullick: 132. Reproduced by permission of the publishers, McCrimmons, Great Wakering, Essex.

© 1992 Kate McIlhagga: from *Encompassing Presence, the Prayer Handbook 1993*, published by the United Reformed Church, 86 Tavistock Place, London WC1H 9RT: 60, 198, 201, 232.

Helena McKinnon: 7.

Nancy Martin: from *Prayers for Children and Young People*, 237.

Janet Morley: from *All Desires Known*, published by SPCK, 26, 153, 191, 199; from *Bread of Tomorrow*, ed. Janet Morley, Christian Aid/ SPCK 1992, 202.

Mowbray: from *Glastonbury Journey*, Brian Frost, 97, 212.

Reproduced from *Oceans of Prayer*, published by the National Christian Education Council: Maureen Edwards and Jan S. Pickard, 47, 48–49, 53, 68, 71, 136, 144, 224, 225, 249, 251, 252–53, 256–57.

Janet Nightingale: from *Bread of Tomorrow*, ed. Janet Morley, Christian Aid/SPCK 1992, 247.

Mary Oakley: from *A Day at a Time*, 109, 131, by permission.

Alison O'Grady: from *Encounters, the Prayer Handbook 1988*, published by the United Reformed Church, 12.

Copyright © Judith B. O'Neill, 1955: from *Rejoice and Sing*, 206–7.

Oxford University Press: from *Rejoice and Sing*, 37.

Adelaide A. Procter: from *Rejoice and Sing*, 250.

Random House UK Limited: from *Loving Promises*, Helen Steiner Rice, 114, 182.

Bridget Rees: from *Bread of Tomorrow*, ed. Janet Morley, Christian Aid/SPCK 1992, 75.

Josephine Robertson: from *Prayers for the Later Years*, published by Abingdon Press, 154, 178.

SCM Press Ltd: from *The School of Prayer*, Olive Wyon, 89.

Scottish Academic Press: from *Carmina Gadelica*, 107, 186, 205.

Scripture Press: from Evelyn Christenson, *What Happens When Women Pray*, Victor Books, 15, 33, 85, 86, 98.

Used by permission of Scripture Union: from *Alive to God*, Jan-Mar 1993, Sister Gillian Mary S.S.C., 21, from *Alive to God*, Jan-Mar 1992, Jane Grayshon, 94, Veronica Zundel, 133, 148, Patsy Kettle, 106, from *Alive to God*, Apr-Jun 1992, Jenny Peterson, 66, 200, from *Alive to God*, Jan-Mar 1991, Angela Reith, 54, from *Alive to God*, Apr-Jun 1990, Alison White, 30, from *Alive to God*, Jul-Sept 1990, Kathy Keay, 29, 119, Veronica Zundel, 123.

Sheed & Ward: from *The True Prayers of St. Gertrude and St. Mechtilde*, translated by Canon John Gray, 116, 149, from *The Queen's Daughters*, C.C. Martindale S.J., 141.

Mavis Ford and D. and L. Binion, © Springtide/Word Music (UK)/administered by Copycare Ltd 1978: 52.

D. Helen Stone: from *Congregational Praise*, 151.

Margaret T. Taylor: from *Encounters, the Prayer Handbook 1998*, published by the United Reformed Church, 126.

Margaret Tottle: 254.

K.A. Trimakas S. J. (translator): from *Prayers written by Lithuanian prisoners in Northern Siberia*, 138.

Victor Gollancz: from *A Prison, A Paradise*, Loren Hurnscot, 127.

Susan Williams: from *Lord of Our World, Modern Collects from the Gospels*, published by Falcon: 128, 204, from *Prayers for Today's Church*, Dick Williams, published by Falcon: 158.

Women's World Day of Prayer: 11, 28, 36, 217, 234, Jean Bryan, 3, Mrs Rathie Selvaratnam (1968), 221, 226, Women of Africa (1969), 121, Women of Australia (1986), 96, Women of Brazil (1988), 220, 227, 235, 243, Women of Burma (1989), 222–23, 236, Women of Canada (1978), 215, 229, Women of the Caribbean (1983), 233, Women of Czechoslovakia (1990), 239, Women of East Germany (1977), 34, Women of Guatemala (1993), 216, Women of Ireland (1982), 238, Women of Jamaica

(1971), 25, 120, 211, Women of Japan (1974) 213, 218, Women of Kenya (1991), 18, Women of Mexico (1976), 219, 242, Women of New Zealand (1973), 9, 40, 103, 122, 137, Women of Sweden (1984), 230–31, Women of Thailand (1980), 118, 181, Women of Uruguay (1962), 113.

Taken from *Women Who Do Too Much* by Patricia H. Sprinkle, copyright © 1992 by Patricia Sprinkle. Used by permission of Zondervan Publishing House: 147; taken from *The Five Silent Years of Corrie ten Boom* by Pamela Rosewell, copyright © 1986 by The Zondervan Corporation. Used by permission of Zondervan Publishing House: 67.